Ghost(ed) Woman
& the Electric Purple Pants

Also by Emilie Lindemann

Dear Minimum Wage Employee, You Are Priceless

Queen of the Milky Way

Lost & Found, with artist Karen Laudon

Small Adult Trees / Small Adulteries

mother-mailbox

Nesting, with artist Erin LaBonte

Capsule Wardrobe for the End of the World

Rupture Readings, with artist Karen Laudon

Ghost(ed) Woman
& the Electric Purple Pants

Poems

by

Emilie Lindemann

Fresh Water Press

Two Rivers, Wisconsin

Printed in the United States of America

Fresh Water Press
P.O. Box 425
Two Rivers, WI

Cover design by Vagabond Creative Studio

Cover art: *You Are the Peace You Seek,* by Ginny Laukka.
Oil on Linen. 2024.
Used by kind permission of the artist.

Author photo is by Amy Howarth

ISBN: 979-8-9912318-4-8

Library of Congress Control Number: 2025936117

Dedication

For my colleagues and students from the Before Times.

We never really got to say goodbye.

*

For anyone who has ever experienced the rug being pulled out from under them.

*

For those who feel most seen and most like themselves when wearing an unusual piece of clothing or accessories.

Table of Contents

Ghost(ed) Woman 13

After losing her job during Covid-19… 14

In a Hollow Tree 15

Ghost(ed) Woman with Portals 17

Ghost(ed) Woman with Library Caramels 18

Ghost(ed) Woman Scans Her Notebook 19

Ghost(ed) Woman Leaves a Library Note 20

When she pouts in the bathtub, ... 21

Looking at a Map of the Former Office, Now Demolished 22

Dreamscape//with amaretto latte as time travel portal 23

Inspired by that Time Travel Scene in *Lucy,* You Retrace Your

Steps to Find a Blue Heron 24

Time Cleaning// Arctic Wash 25

Dreamscape// Pandemic Travel via Horizontal Silage 26

Dreamscape//with static 27

At the end of an NPR article, someone casually mentions that

time and space are probably an illusion 28

Dreamscape//on thrifted ice skates 29

Trying 30

I went to Reykjavík in my sleep 31

Peonies, finally, ... 32

Dreamscape//with "You are safe" painted rock talisman 34

Dreamscape// Visible Wind Patterns 36

4 Portals for Winter Darkness 37

Fragments while biking & being mistaken for a clover 39

Two mediums predict when I finish my cold brew. 41

Almost May again 42

Acknowledgements 44

Ghost(ed) Woman

Last seen wearing oversized sunglasses reminiscent of the mid aughts. Last seen waving a brisk goodbye to the job that melted like coconut oil (or is she more of a butter girl? Has she ever used lard?). She likes other people's posts as if to leave croutons to the edge of some wooded area, her keystrokes hitting the screen in ghost time.

She extracts unrequited emails and lets them dry out in a cool, dark place. Herbs waiting, no expiration, no best by date. When Gmail says *sent 7 days ago. Follow up?*, she drifts under a pine tree, its branches extending over the sidewalk to the library. She finds a cart of philosophy books and feels the purple and deep blue spines and covers. Feels her toes, root-like, anchoring her to the tile floor of the library's vestibule.

There is never a reply.

After losing her job during Covid-19…

She finds a four-leaf clover
and in between bouts of panic but before
of lavender in two years. The clover she presses
the cover and sees the dizzy passing of decades
tumbling or maybe all those squares

bedecked interiors that she scrolled through
decades, they'd spin ahead, a digital whirligig
open the book again. Holding the clover
no clover would beckon. Maybe no person
way. Perhaps she would be known for

while sprawled on the hill during magic hour
harvesting the thickest bundle
in a book—a biography of Dickinson. She shuts
like couch cushions of a make-shift fort
with photos of contoured faces, garland-

most nights. Before-and-after bodies. Those
you use to find your birthdate and then she'd
to her cheek. Forgetting or remembering, maybe
would think of her as a writer or in any poet-like
her rainboots or for her silence.

Her
silence
sighing,
a sort
of soaring
    or
singing.

In a Hollow Tree

Lately, I've been thinking

about hollow trees,   about

a door that I didn't see.

"Where is his mom?"

my son asks,

every time I read the book to him

about a rabbit named Nicholas

who sleeps in the most secure, *hygge*

            hollow space.

I'm in hiding, stowing acorns

in with my Flair pens//

burrowing in my wood-paneled nest.

In the office for ghosts:

no personal effects,

not even empty coffee mugs.

{Except for a teapot motif umbrella

for a few rainy weeks}

The key creaks

in the lock//

The truth is,

I would teach here

in this office for ghosts

just to have *somewhere* to go.

Ghost(ed) Woman with Portals

She was drawn to cupboards

that were open just a crack,

        doorknobs with locks

        that had been painted over.

No matter where she went

in that oak-tree canopied place,

        she was left pacing

        on layers of wet leaves in hallways,

looking for a cubby hole that she could nest in if needed,

somewhere to exist quietly.

Ghost(ed) Woman with Library Caramels

The woman in the pink wool coat

says no one hears the crinkles

of her library caramels.

    Or her bootsteps on the concrete

    of the echoey pavilion before the woods.

If you listened to her pockets,

you'd hear phantom pens

    etching

desperate adjunct instructor notes in polyester lining.

    If you can see me, she whispers,

holding out a caramel

with a cream center.

    Or is it an acorn?

Ghost(ed) Woman Scans Her Notebook

When she checks again,

    a staircase appears.

On the second floor, she sees a long wooden table—

    perfect for a ghost with a filigreed notebook.

Her stainless-steel water bottle thuds

onto the wooden surface.

    "Sorry,"

she whispers to the emptiness.

A bulletin board upstairs uses text language

to ask, *wht r u wrtng?*

    It takes her a long time to reply.

She holds up her notebook and maintains

    a steady gaze,

as if waiting for it to scan.

Ghost(ed) Woman Leaves a Library Note

Until the cupboard won't open.

      Until the snow heaps recede.

Until all those layers of ivory, deep teal, and wine paint.

      Until she is the only one *ever* in the library.

When she writes in deep indigo Sharpie,

only a hint of someone else (some*ones?*)

rustling in the leaves.

If there's no one here to read it,

does this mean…?

When she pouts in the bathtub,

cascades of frothy pink, turquoise blue, and violet water sweep over everything. Like being in a carwash—only, there's no roof or windows. She feels like less of a ghost when she's biking. Her shadow, the movement, the cool gusts of air and the sandhill cranes actually acknowledge her—even if just to rattle a call and flap their wings. If she's lucky, a quick wave to a bevy of swans in the pond. The teal bicycle not unlike the Etch-a-Sketch (travel-sized) that she used to shuttle into sleep when she was a seven-year-old in a bunk bed.

Looking at a Map of the Former Office, Now Demolished

On the page, you didn't see

the ink flowing with its lemony wash.

You thought it was your favorite boulder

at the stream. Is there sound,

or are you watching movement?

You are at your most silent

in the dotted line spaces of a missing room

with a view of a crabapple tree.

You assume said tree still exists,

although who hears it now?

You used to fold

into a velvet library chair

grading papers back in time.

Maybe you are underlining

new streams

beneath such beautiful glimmers

even now

when something missing

should wobble on the page.

Dreamscape//with amaretto latte as time travel portal

I'm in the future wearing a powder blue pants suit and those pale blue heels from my favorite consignment shop. When I look up *amaretto*, I already hear the voice of the stranger from my dream: "Did you say amaretto?" When I google it, I'm in an espresso-stained apron, squirting whipped cream on a towering iced mocha, eating all the crinkle cookies I want as long as the manager doesn't see. In the dream, I'm always worrying, wearing the suit or the apron. No in between. No muskrat-sheltering stream dresses with wild blue phlox hems.

Inspired by that Time Travel Scene in *Lucy,* You Retrace Your Steps to Find a Blue Heron

You were moving too quickly   and skipped a page. Skipped over a whole forest, the soggy log for sitting with the mossy footrest and all. Flew past the room//with all your favorite things, even the high-heeled booties you bought and never wore in public. What kind of occasion would call for sitting whimsically on a bar stool// swooping in for a blue lagoon martini and then getting your left heel stuck in the staircase grating? Swipe back to the woods, pan over to a patch of water, green, in another season. A blue heron stands there, maybe in your suede boots. A reflection pooling in that lime green place you almost didn't see.

Time Cleaning// Arctic Wash

An ocean away

a dusty rose sweater

flaps

on an arctic clothesline.

I'm still here in lilac time

wearing the same cotton shirt

back in 2020 spring.

Blinking and blinking//and blinking

but I can't fly out of the dream.

Dreamscape// Pandemic Travel via Horizontal Silage

That winter, we'd use the plastic-wrapped hay bales to go wherever we wanted. My son balanced atop the tunnel, I jogged on the clover below—snow-covered or otherwise. We'd start in Wisconsin and zip to Paris or Italy, spinning vague movie ideas of tiny tables on cobblestone roads. Baguettes, biscotti, the daintiest cups of coffee. My son never tired of traveling. He didn't want to stay in one spot for long. Maybe a millisecond in Milan. A three-second pause in Peru. It was the motion, the change in location he craved, not those buttery croissants gobbled on the other side. Sometimes we'd only go to Michigan, sometimes New Zealand. Hours and time zones passed in moments, and it was still that winter. I was still jogging from one end of the silage to the other, saying "Careful! Not too fast!" or "Where to next?"

Dreamscape//with static

"You have my antenna, now,"

my grandmother says,

just before she whirs away, a green blur,

her lead foot on the gas pedal of a John Deere Gator.

In the dream, I'm cradling a cordless phone.

When I wake up,

the signal is so weak, I drop the call.

Ssssstttttattttticcccccc.

I've stepped on the phantom curly cord.

Days pass, and she cruises back,

speeding

through swirls of mud.

Where are we going? (should I ask?)

Get in (does she say?)

Taking her antenna,

the ancient cordless phone,

to my itchy ear,

I press my bare foot

where her loafer paused

and fly.

At the end of an NPR article, someone casually mentions that time and space are probably an illusion

She once read about overlapping maps.

Closing her eyes,

in a sunlit yoga studio of the future,

a museum

of sweating furiously, luxuriously.

What she remembers now

is deodorant.

She is here and also

elsewhere

sorting the sculptures

and accepting a cold

eucalyptus towel on the forehead

    through a brick red door

In the museum of sculpture

she crosses through a red door

and tries to remember

This   space

Once, she found a piece

of birthday cake

among the sculptures

It was supposed to stay there,

indefinitely. Did this mean glitter?

When the roof collapsed,

snow overhead, sinking.

Eyes closed, she crosses

all these birthdays later.

Dreamscape//on thrifted ice skates

After a two-decade lapse

I'm dancing

through time

instead of letting it scroll through me.

I shuffle on thrifted blades,

choppy steps at first,

but then swoop-glide and scrape-twirl.

At 39, I am afraid

of the gut-punch of an email,

of skidding and thumping to the hard cold ground.

At another rink

surrounded by cedar trees

where the ice is bumpy & broken

I'm here as I wobble-soar

into snowmelt,

as I glide into dreamtime.

Skate-poems emerge

rough scratches on the ice

and then lopsided flourishes,

swooping

and here.

Trying

Last night, I tried to see the Northern Lights.

Tried to appreciate stars in my plaid winter coat on the hill where my lavender plants hide under snow and dead leaves.

Tried to find peace in the moment, my life only halfway over, if I'm lucky.

I ate some more cheese popcorn and then went back out to look at the stars.

Tried to "cherish every cell in [my] body" like the card I picked at yoga class advised.

Tried to live generously. Tried to avoid shopping too much. Tried to remember to brush my teeth after eating onion-y Greek pasta salad.

Plaid winter coats only last until the fabric gives out, and even then, with a little mending, what is and isn't eternity?

I try to walk to the woods with some regularity, swishing through a half-frozen mat of oak leaves and wondering (not worrying) what will come next.

I went to Reykjavík in my sleep

Palest gray & periwinkle// bleak

& sun-dazzled// spilled

water on the carpeting

carrying firewood in for the night.

I budge open a thick wooden door

with round glass peepholes

in cobalt blue, red, gold, green.

On the other side, I'm already in Reykjavik,

scrolling back before the virus

when stained glass paintings glowed

inside the café

whose reddish-brown carpeting// well-worn,

holds us.

I wonder if I'll ever taste it

or if my closest reach

is through this screen

savoring

every square of the waffles

//saturated

with jam and cream.

Peonies, finally,

& someone exhaled

a river, too—cobalt blue.

Someone's breath full of bloom.

A deep, dense forest—

I thought of rosebush leaves

or I stopped thinking, finally,

& became//peony air,

became peony mind,

big and blooming.

Every pink petal

tendered air.

The kind HR manager's voice:

...*by a thread*

...*other candidates.*

Pixelated pompons

patched in over my blankness.

In peony time,

waves and woods both accepted me,

said, *there's an opening,*

said, *you.*

Dreamscape//with "You are safe" painted rock talisman

The smooth stone

sighs its painted letters & puffy clouds:

"You are safe. You are safe.

You are safe."

Your anxiety-brain

catches up a few bites

of a peanut butter cookie remnant later.

You brush the crumbs across

a rose-motif quilt

onto the late summer grass.

Months later, you'll grip the cool stone

in your wood-paneled make-shift office,

a wall of books rainbowed behind you.

Awkward zoom teaching chatter before class starts—

your voice too high, too fast.

The painted rock says,

"You are safe. You are safe.

You are safe."

A blue Frisbee's soar,

a wall of cocooning cedar trees,

the feel

of an olive-green linen dress

on the knees—

or lake effect breeze.

Dreamscape// Visible Wind Patterns

On a weekend of below zero wind gusts, you mother two
houseplants from Lowe's, hoping they survive. You draw wind
swirl after wind swirl while the pages of your notebook exhale out
of your mouth. You are grateful for their company, the vine swirls
mimicking every wind drawing you make with colored pencil. The
mauve plastic planter matches your favorite colored pencil, and
you're having trouble connecting with humans right now. It's not
just olive green swirl, blue ink swirl, fuchsia pencil swirl. You are
making motions and listening to the blasts. Breezes. Bursts.
Torrents. Gales. Whooshes. Whirls. Squalls. Puffs. Drafts. Just
trying to pick up the language. Just trying to reach tendril to tendril.

4 Portals for Winter Darkness

1.

These blizzard days

bring back pandemic days,

& I make the same everything

bagels with half cream cheese,

half blueberry jam. A basil

nectarine candle flickers

just before the power goes out.

2.

In the graphite spaces

between the lattice fence,

clusters of stars

in a blurry winter sky.

The entire flock of us

flapping

and struggling

then darting through and out.

3.

A slab

of raspberry vanilla cream cake

appears the next day, a small token

from a missed family party.

Surprise snowdrifts keeping us trapped

and alone.

4.

After inching along the ice

on a 7 below zero night,

a hot paper bag

delivered with kindness

at the end of this January drive-thru.

Fragments while biking & being mistaken for a clover

*

The Queen Anne's lace and chicory are ushering her down the road.
She is flying via bicycle again, standing up and coasting.
Later, there will be a half moon visible
in the still-light sky. A jarringly orange Monarch
flattened beneath the stop sign. She brakes, squeakily.
Every summer new poems that smell of fresh-water waves
& wild raspberries. Something pilfers her courage
before she can properly dust these words.

*

At the far end of her rural road, there's a stream on one side
and an expansive pond on the other. Primroses in June,
a turtle on the side of the road now and then.
A cigarette carton that someone has discarded.
Without trying to be beautiful, a lone pelican pauses.

*

She is tired of trying to be beautiful. Everything feels watched
and counted. For months, she gleefully left her purple Fitbit stagnant
on the kitchen counter. No one has bothered to count
such tiny toads in the early July grass.

*

Savoring almond croissants all winter {and spring}, she never
worried about getting lost in the intricacies of Queen Anne's lace.
That July, the lilies had already opened.

*

How it feels to inhale rosemary or grapefruit
from those tiny bottles at the salon. The exact hue of the tiger lilies
at her grandmother's house. Lake Michigan at Point Creek.
All those stones under her feet and how she once swam
to the silky sand bar. She doesn't want to lose this feeling.

*

Writing in bed, listening to distant fireworks, she is a pelican
or a tiny toad. The next day, biking again in green yoga pants
and a pinkish top, a Monarch flies between her elbow and torso,
mistaking her for the clover she truly is.

Two mediums predict when I finish my cold brew.

One wears all black, stretchy fabrics. The other has a teal skirt like lake water under the darkest night sky. They stir teacups without ever looking in my direction. Between sips, they lower their voices and shield their energy from the jittery ghosts spinning and spinning on the yellow vinyl stools at the coffee bar. In the alley way, pink and purple petunias bloom and fade in seconds. Two alien mediums drain their champagne glasses, after toasting soundlessly, their eyes still on the pair inside.

Almost May again

Are these still

my poems

if this all ends with me

clawing out of the   hollow

tree in early May, | Rain- | negotiating with HR

across a rain-soaked   speckled   weekend while silence elapses?

I tell myself I am   allowed to succeed as long as//

(what)?   window

I am not sure where   the boundaries are,

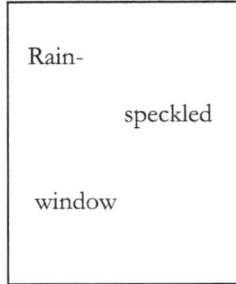

only that once, sipping red wine, I asked someone if they also get scared

when good things happen.

[.]

I blink at my ceiling, trying to send a message

to the ghosted woman I was

that year.

She sees it now on the bulletin board,

the library's second floor where she is invisible

except when she wears electric purple pants.

Acknowledgements

I wish to thank the editors of the following literary journals where some of the poems in this chapbook first appeared:

Art as Poetry as Art Exhibition (2020-2024): "Looking at a Map of the Former Office, Now Demolished," "Fragments while biking and being mistaken for a clover," "Inspired by that Time Travel Scene in Lucy, You Retrace Your Steps to Find a Blue Heron," and "4 Portals for Winter Darkness"

Bramble: "After losing her job during Covid-19..." and "Dreamscape//with amaretto latte as time travel portal"

Center for 21st Century Studies, Lonely No More Online Exhibit: "Dreamscape// Visible Wind Patterns"

FERAL: "Dreamscape// Pandemic Travel via Horizontal Sileage"

Hummingbird Magazine of the Short Poem: "Time Cleaning// Arctic Wash"*

Sequestrum: "Ghost(ed) Woman," "In a Hollow Tree," and "When she pouts in the bathtub"

Vividly [a pamphlet and exhibit featuring poetry that connects with the theme of mental health hosted by John Michael Kohler Arts Center]: "Dreamscape//with 'You are Safe' Painted Rock Talisman"

Wandering Toft Point: a Journal: "Peonies, finally"

I'm so thankful for the care that Fresh Water Press editor and publisher Peggy Turnbull put into transforming this manuscript into a book. Peggy, you understood exactly what these poems were about and knew that the visual elements contribute to the whole reading experience. Thank you to you and your partners at FWP, Tara Huck and Tracey Koach, for providing just the right home for this chapbook. Thank you, Sophia Dramm, for your wisdom on editing short-form video. I'm so grateful for what Fresh Water Press does to celebrate writing in the lakeshore community and beyond.

Thank you to artist Ginny Laukka for creating a painting that took my breath away and made me feel understood. My thanks also to Vagabond Creative Studio for dreaming up so many cover design variations; you made it difficult to choose just one.

My gratitude to CX Dillhunt and C. Kubasta for offering generous words of support for this chapbook!

Theresa Falvey-Hunt's yoga classes provided joy, connection, and perspective during a time when I needed this most. Sarah Sadie's creative prompts and online community likely nurtured several of these poems. Thank you!

Thank you to my friends and family for your love and support. Steve Sukowaty, you are my voice of reason and my rock. Oliver, your curiosity and creativity inspire me every day. I'd like to thank my parents as well. My father has nurtured an interest in themes of time travel (he's the one who encouraged me to watch *Lucy*), and my mother's love for bold, bright colors must have rubbed off on me. Thank you, Bethany Spalding and Amy Howarth, for always asking about my creative projects and for cheering me on and inspiring me. Thanks also to Maureen Sukowaty, Elise Minard, Noelle Ott, Noah Lindemann, Hope Bair, Faith Pflum, Bart Lindemann Jr., Jonah Lindemann, Susanna Lindemann, and Vienna Lindemann.

---

*The image of the rose pink sweater flapping on the arctic clothesline is inspired by an image from a February 2022 post on the Visit Greenland Instagram page.

Emilie Lindemann is the author of *mother-mailbox* (Misty Publications, 2016) as well as several chapbooks, including *Capsule Wardrobe for the End of the World* (dancing girl press, 2019). She holds a PhD in English-Creative Writing from UW-Milwaukee and teaches writing and communication courses at Lakeshore College. She also serves as a poetry editor for *Stoneboat Literary Journal.* Emilie lives on a dairy farm in Wisconsin with her husband, son, and border collie. Her days are lined with lavender, chicory root, Queen Anne's lace, and red clover.

The Fresh Water Press was founded February 2024 in Two Rivers, Wisconsin, and specializes in books by writers who live in or write about the northeastern Wisconsin lakeshore. The Press publishes in several genres and welcomes submissions from underrepresented authors and unique voices.

Titles from Fresh Water Press:

Opening Nights: A Collection of Theater Stories

Ghost(ed) Woman & the Electric Purple Pants by Emilie Lindemann

Dial Down: Holistic Strategies to Move from Chaos to Calm by Raquel Durden

Radio Starr by Lisa Lehmann